Trace Letter - A

Uppercase

Lowercase

A is for Ant

Trace Letter - B

Uppercase

b
Lowercase

B is for Bee

Trace Letter - C

Uppercase

Lowercase

C is for Cat

Trace Letter - D

Uppercase

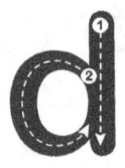
Lowercase

D is for Dog

Trace Letter - E

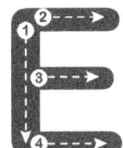
Uppercase

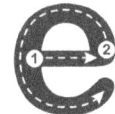
Lowercase

E is for Elephant

Trace Letter - F

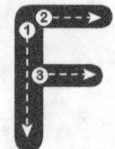

Uppercase

Lowercase

F is for Fox

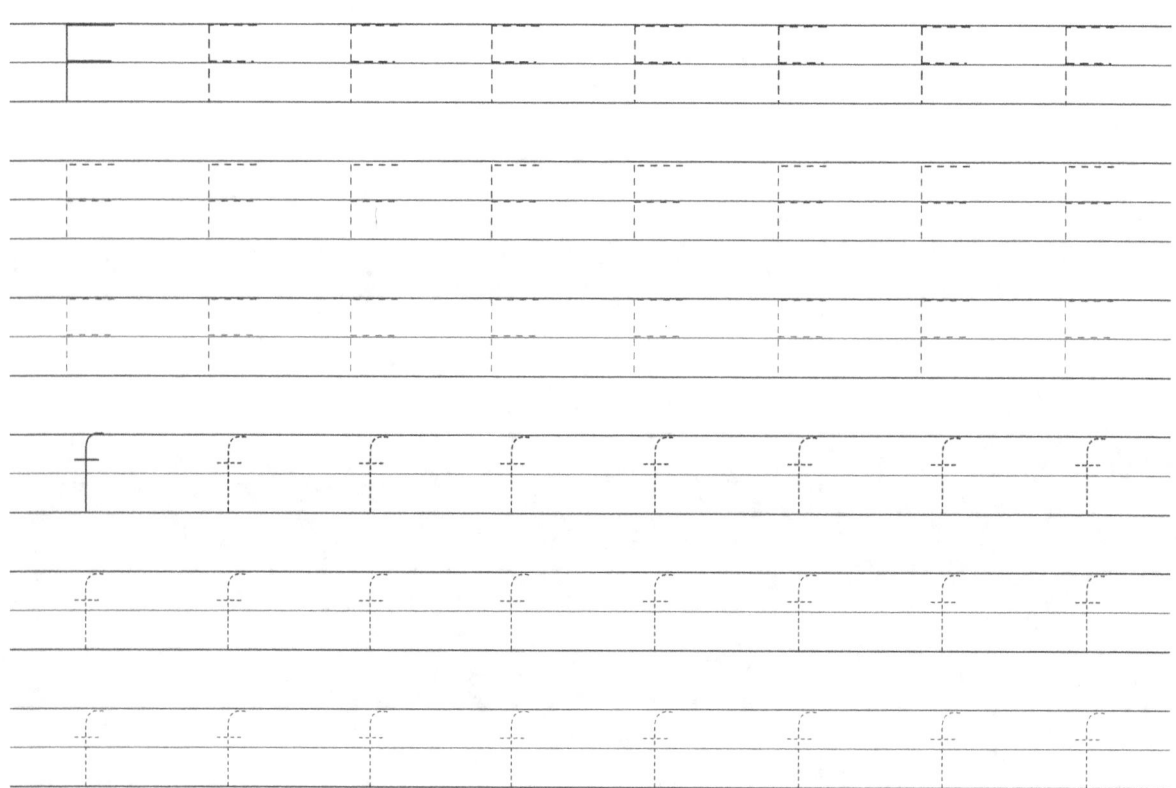

Trace Letter - G

Uppercase

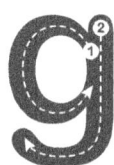
Lowercase

G is for Goat

Trace Letter - H

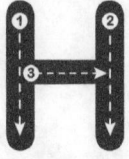
Uppercase

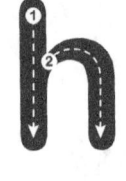
Lowercase

H is for Hippo

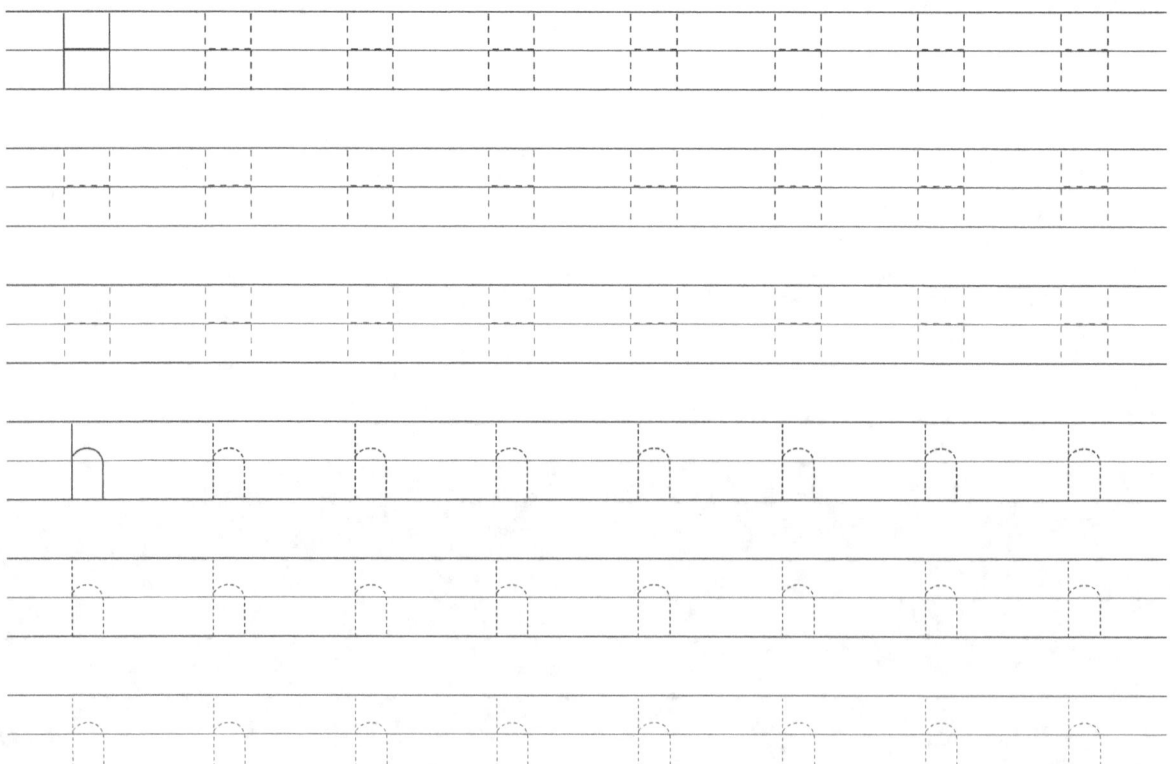

Trace Letter - I

Uppercase

Lowercase

I is for Iguana

Trace Letter - J

Uppercase

Lowercase

J is for Jaguar

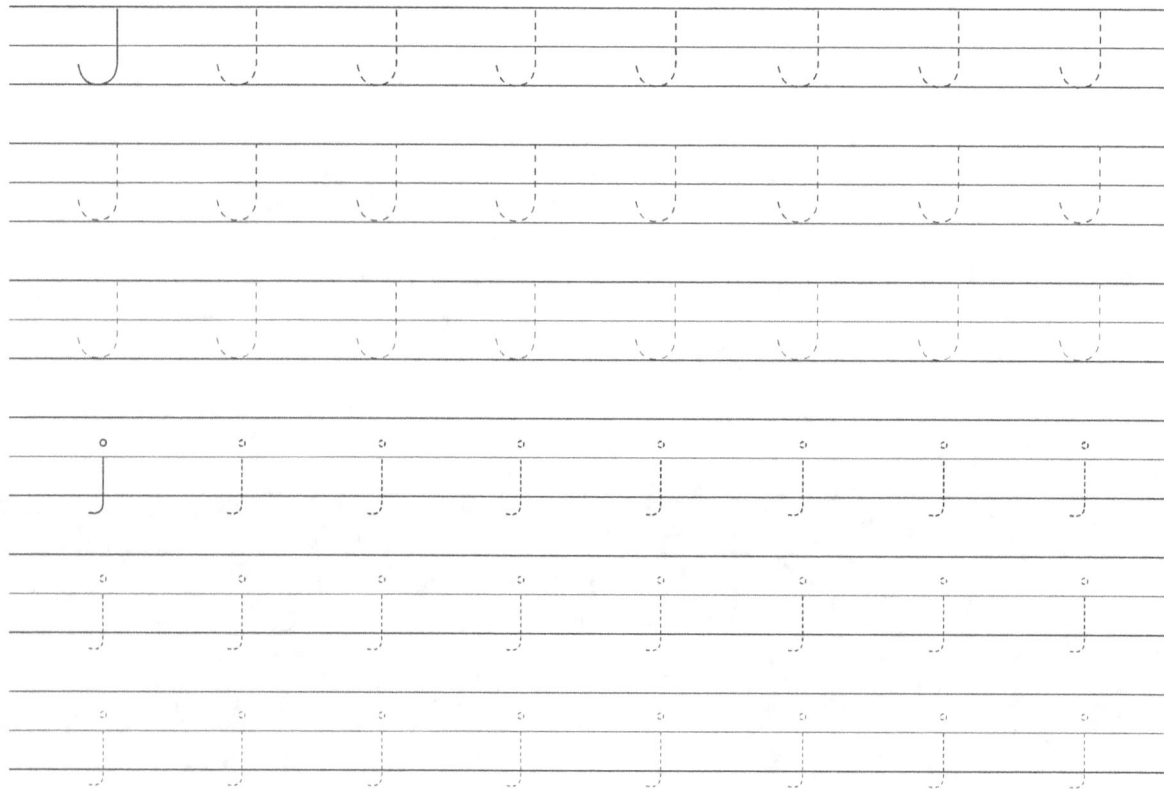

Trace Letter - K

Uppercase

Lowercase

K is for Koala

Trace Letter - L

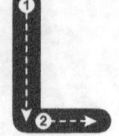

Uppercase

Lowercase

L is for Lion

Trace Letter - M

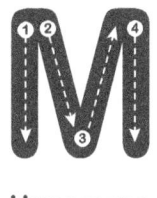
Uppercase

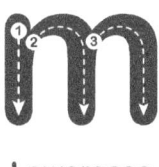
Lowercase

M is for Monkey

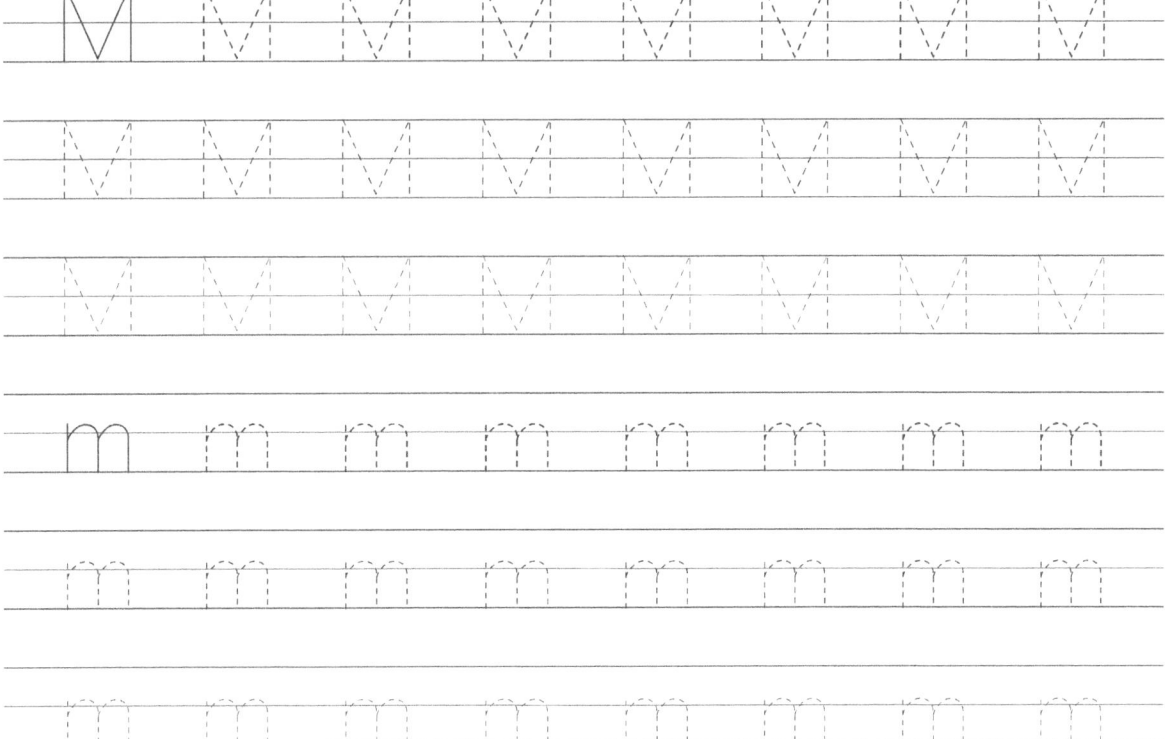

Trace Letter - N

Uppercase

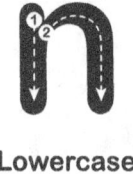
Lowercase

N is for Nightingale

Trace Letter - O

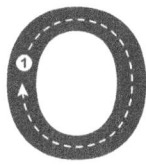
Uppercase

Lowercase

O is for Owl

Trace Letter - P

Uppercase

Lowercase

P is for Penguin

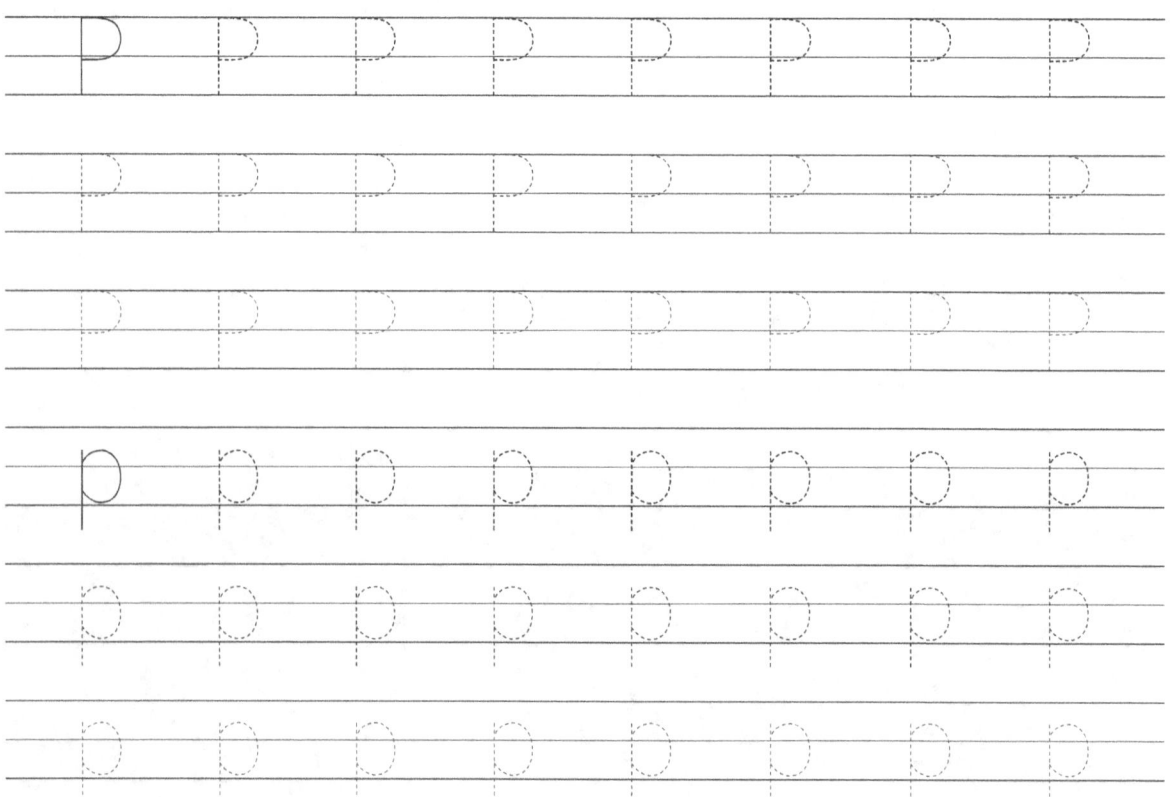

Trace Letter – Q

Uppercase

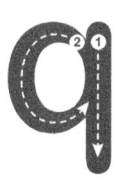
Lowercase

Q is for Quokka

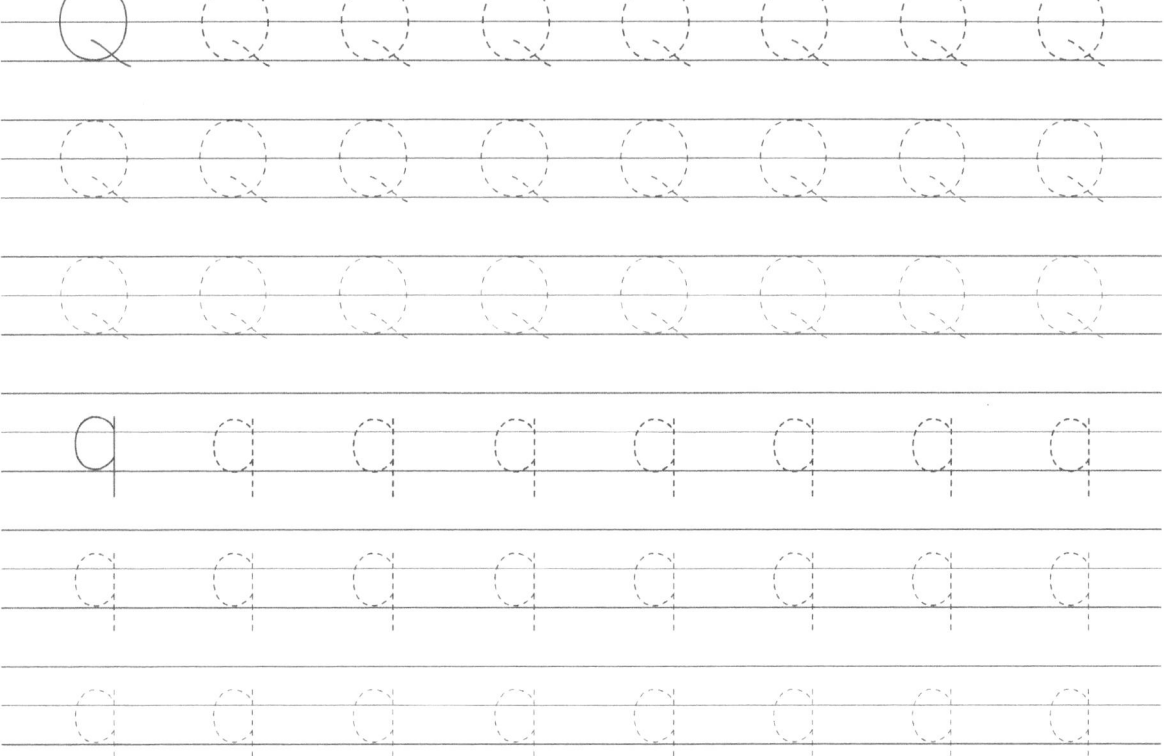

Trace Letter - R

Uppercase

Lowercase

R is for Raccoon

Trace Letter - S

Uppercase

S
Lowercase

S is for Sheep

Trace Letter - T

Uppercase

Lowercase

T is for Toucan

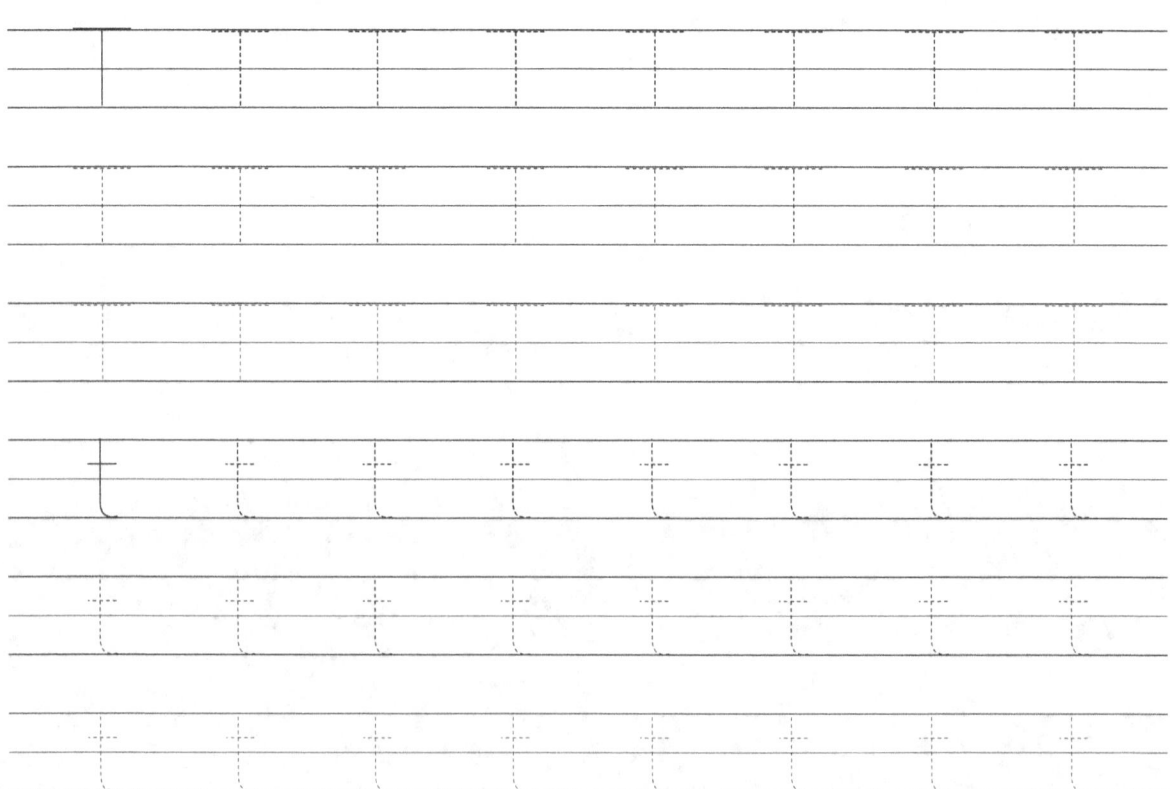

Trace Letter - U

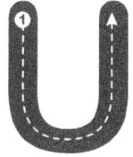
Uppercase

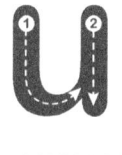
Lowercase

U is for Unicorn

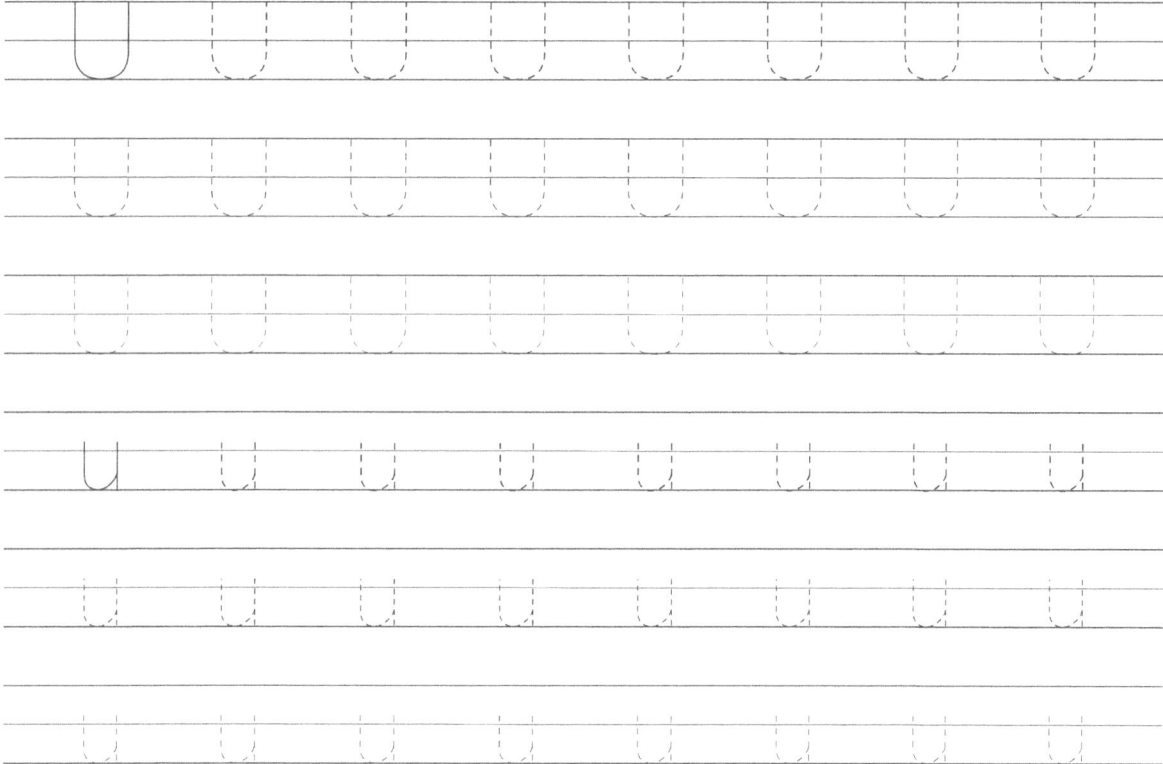

Trace Letter - V

Uppercase

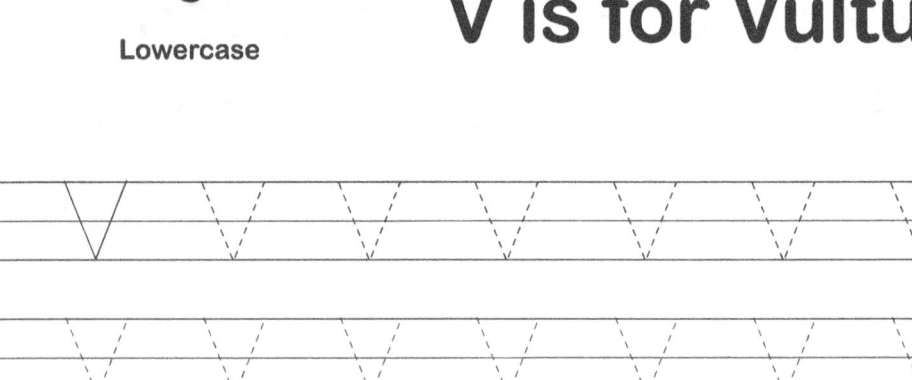
Lowercase

V is for Vulture

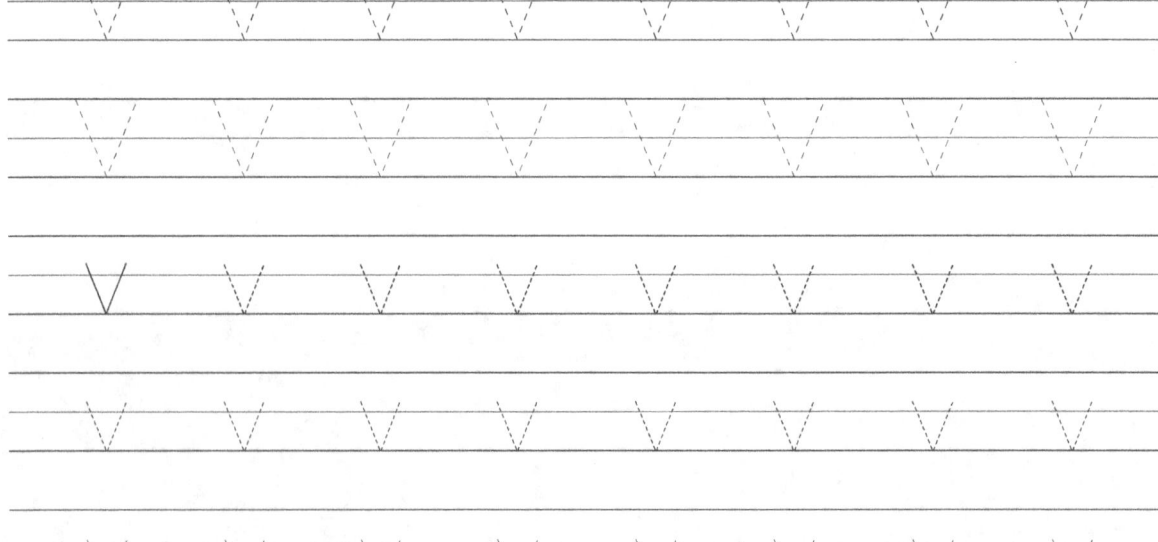

Trace Letter - W

Uppercase

W is for Whale

Trace Letter - X

Uppercase

Lowercase

X is for X-ray fish

Trace Letter - Y

Uppercase

Lowercase

Y is for Yak

Trace Letter - Z

Uppercase

Lowercase

Z is for Zebra

Trace Letter - A

Uppercase

Lowercase

A is for Ant

Trace Letter - B

Uppercase

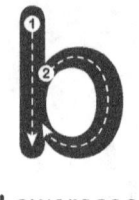

Lowercase

B is for Bee

Trace Letter - C

Uppercase

Lowercase

C is for Cat

Trace Letter - D

Uppercase

Lowercase

D is for Dog

Trace Letter - E

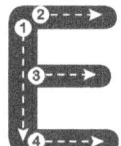
Uppercase

Lowercase

E is for Elephant

Trace Letter - F

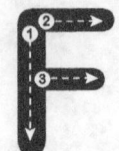

Uppercase

Lowercase

F is for Fox

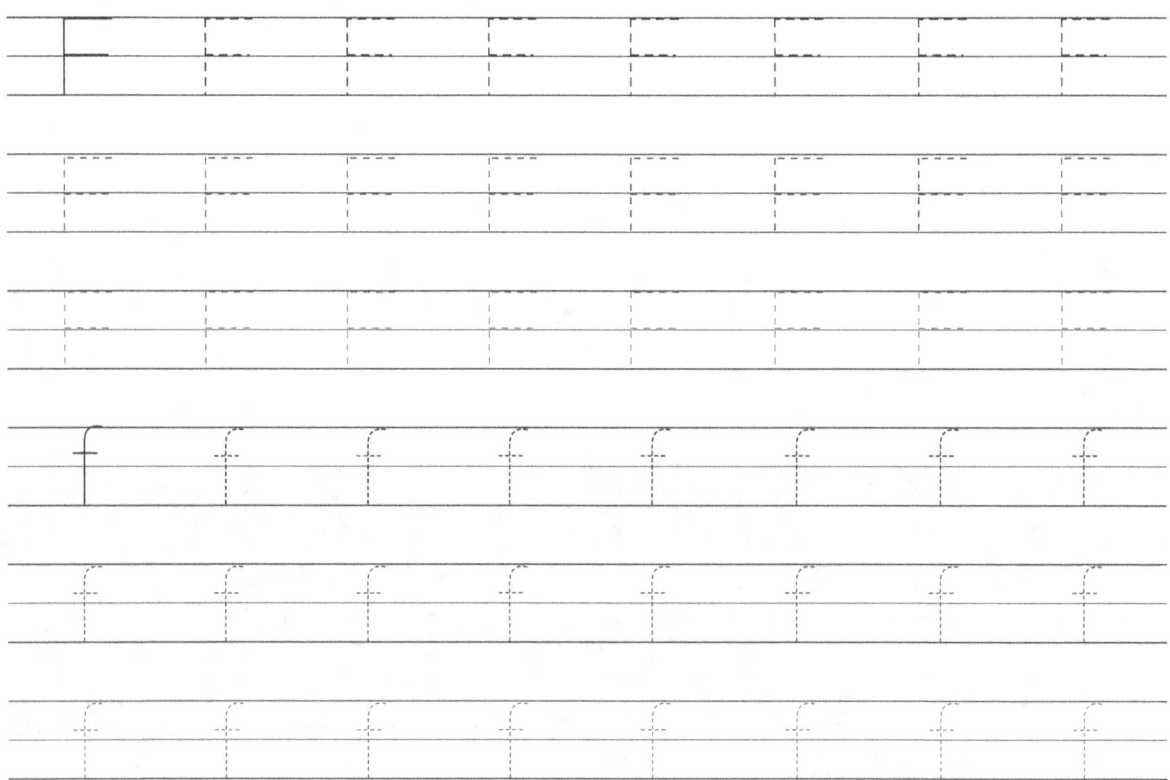

Trace Letter – G

Uppercase

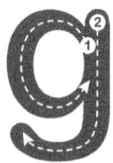
Lowercase

G is for Goat

Trace Letter - H

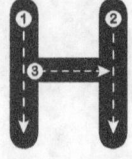
Uppercase

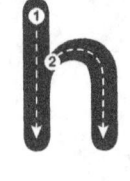
Lowercase

H is for Hippo

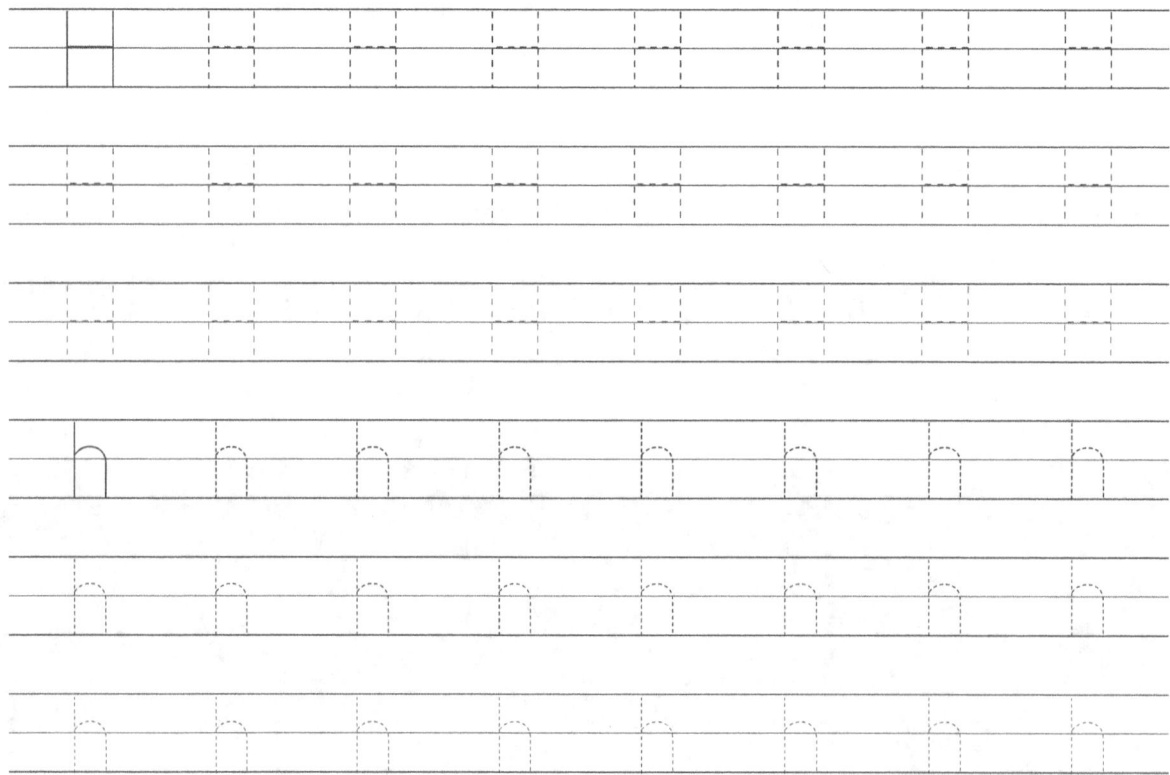

Trace Letter - I

Uppercase

Lowercase

I is for Iguana

Trace Letter - J

Uppercase

Lowercase

J is for Jaguar

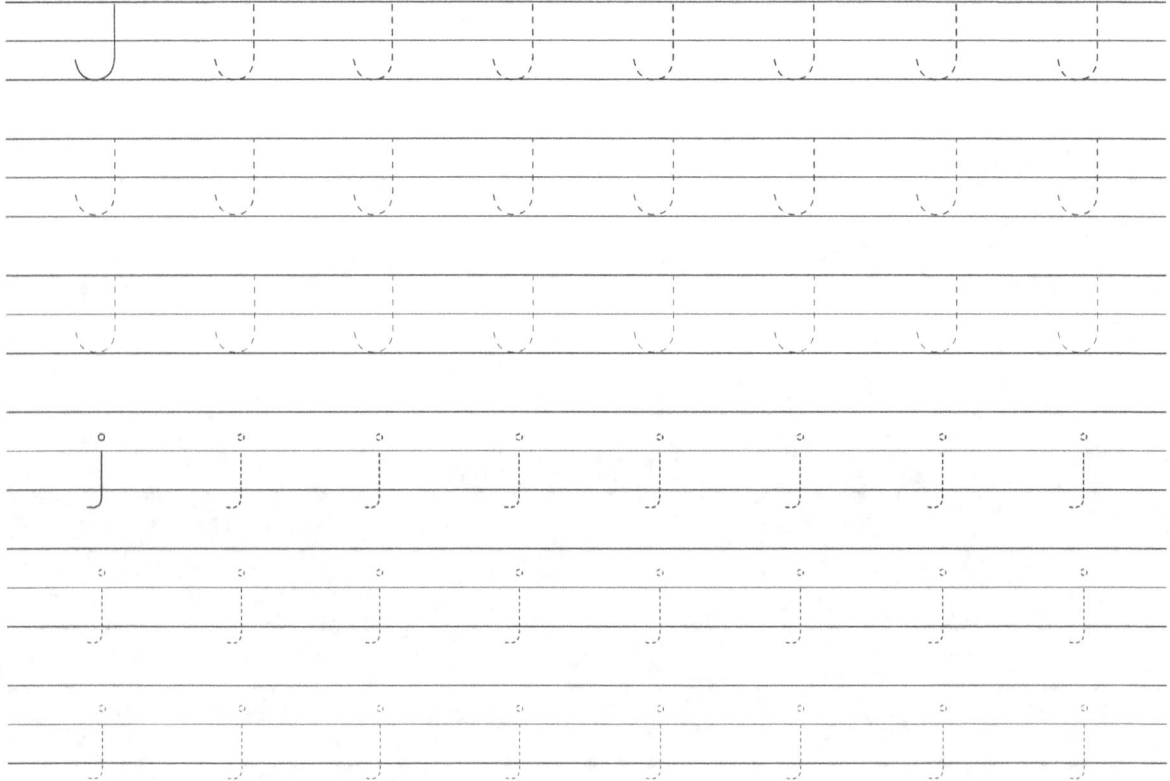

Trace Letter - K

Uppercase

k
Lowercase

K is for Koala

Trace Letter - L

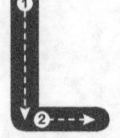
Uppercase

Lowercase

L is for Lion

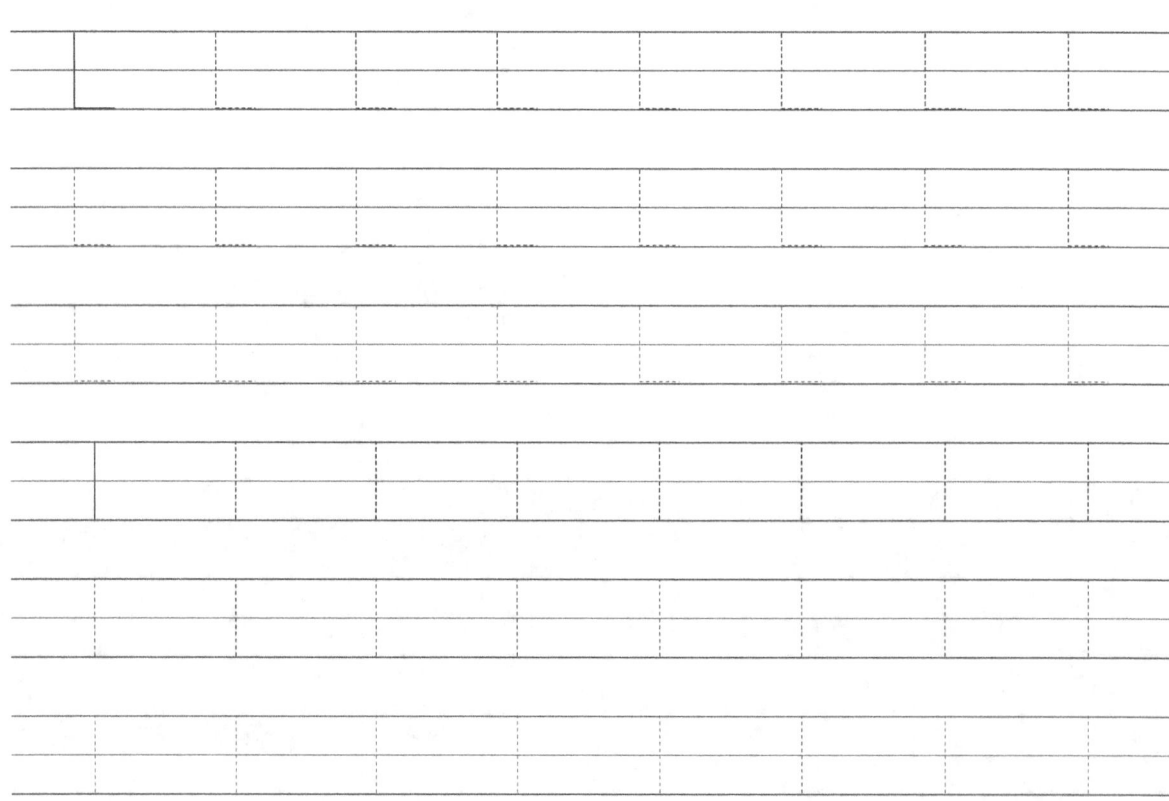

Trace Letter - M

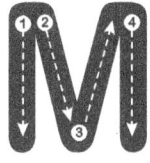

Uppercase

M is for Monkey

Lowercase

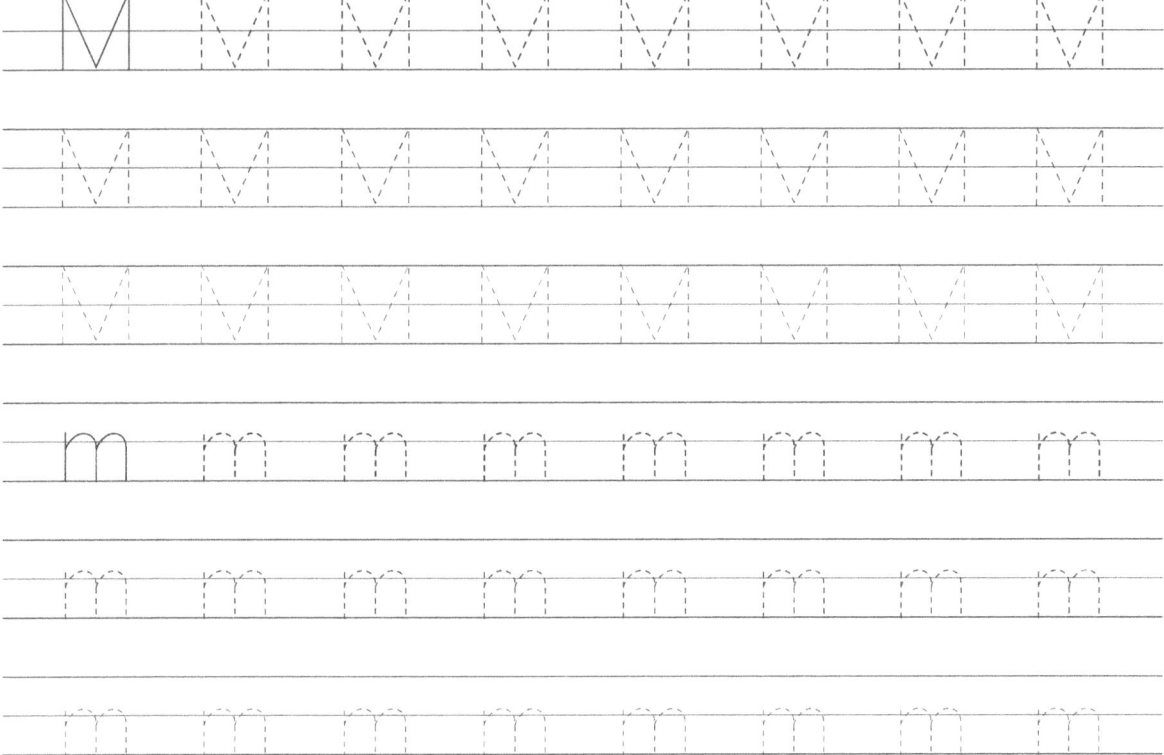

Trace Letter - N

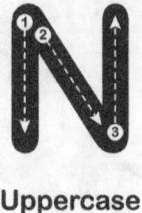
Uppercase

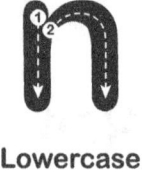
Lowercase

N is for Nightingale

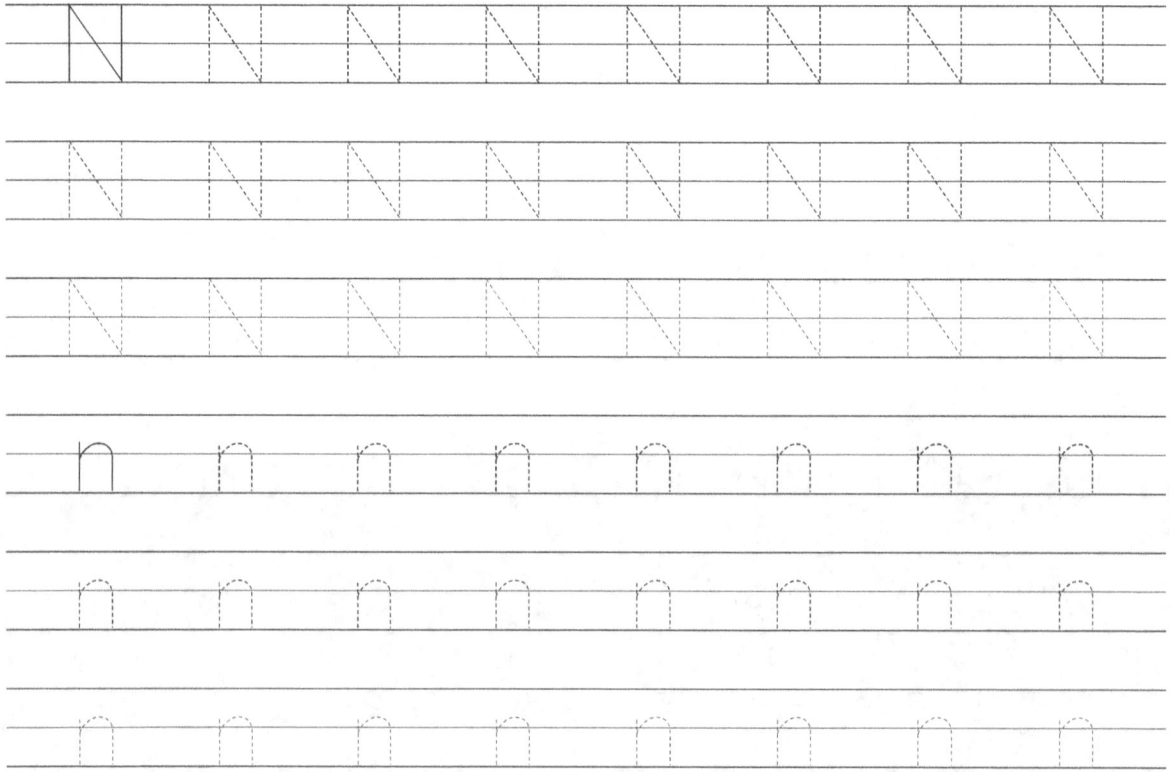

Trace Letter - O

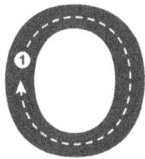
Uppercase

Lowercase

O is for Owl

Trace Letter - P

Uppercase

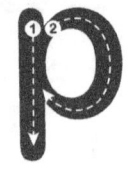
Lowercase

P is for Penguin

Trace Letter - Q

Uppercase

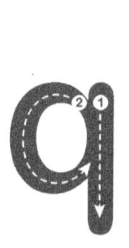
Lowercase

Q is for Quokka

Trace Letter - R

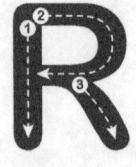
Uppercase

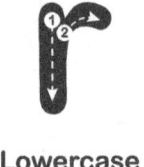
Lowercase

R is for Raccoon

R R R R R R R

R R R R R R R

R R R R R R R

r r r r r r r

r r r r r r r

r r r r r r r

Trace Letter - S

Uppercase

S

Lowercase

S is for Sheep

Trace Letter - T

Uppercase

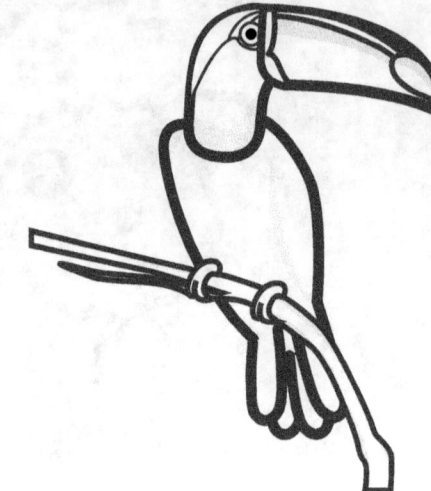

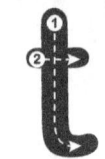
Lowercase

T is for Toucan

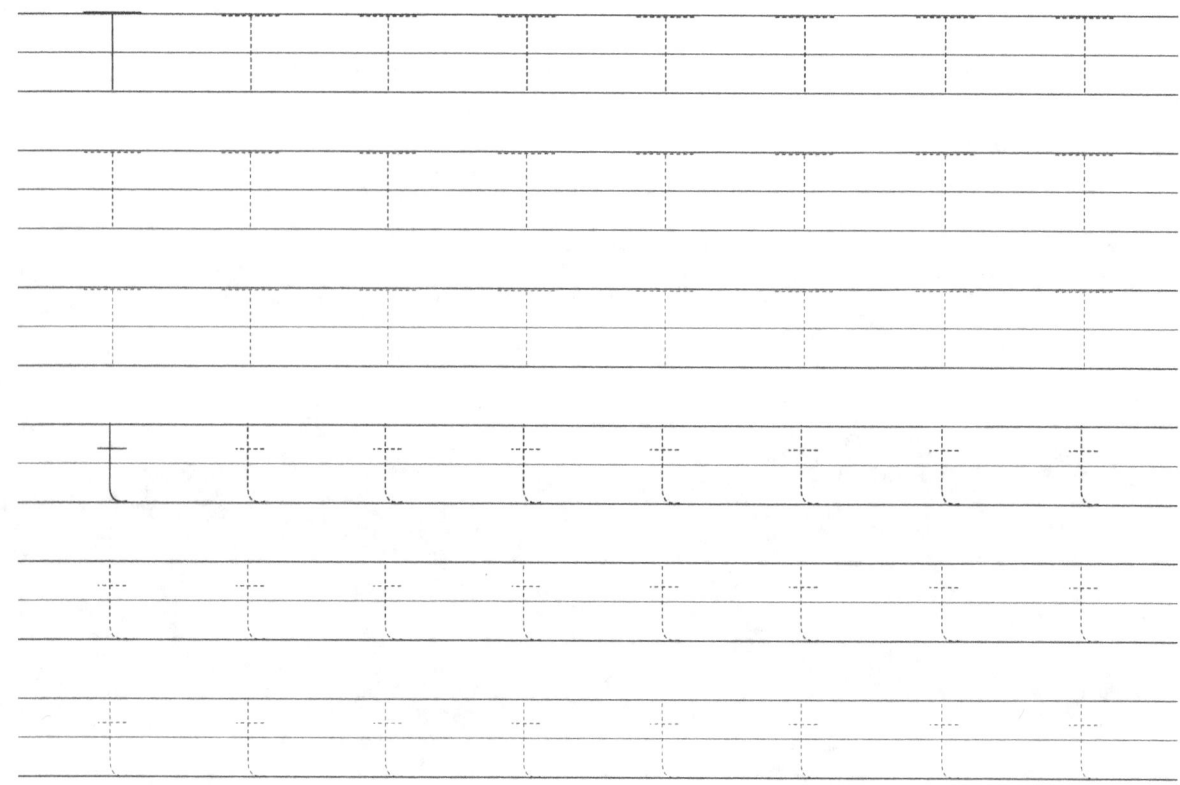

Trace Letter - U

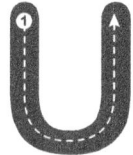
Uppercase

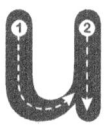
Lowercase

U is for Unicorn

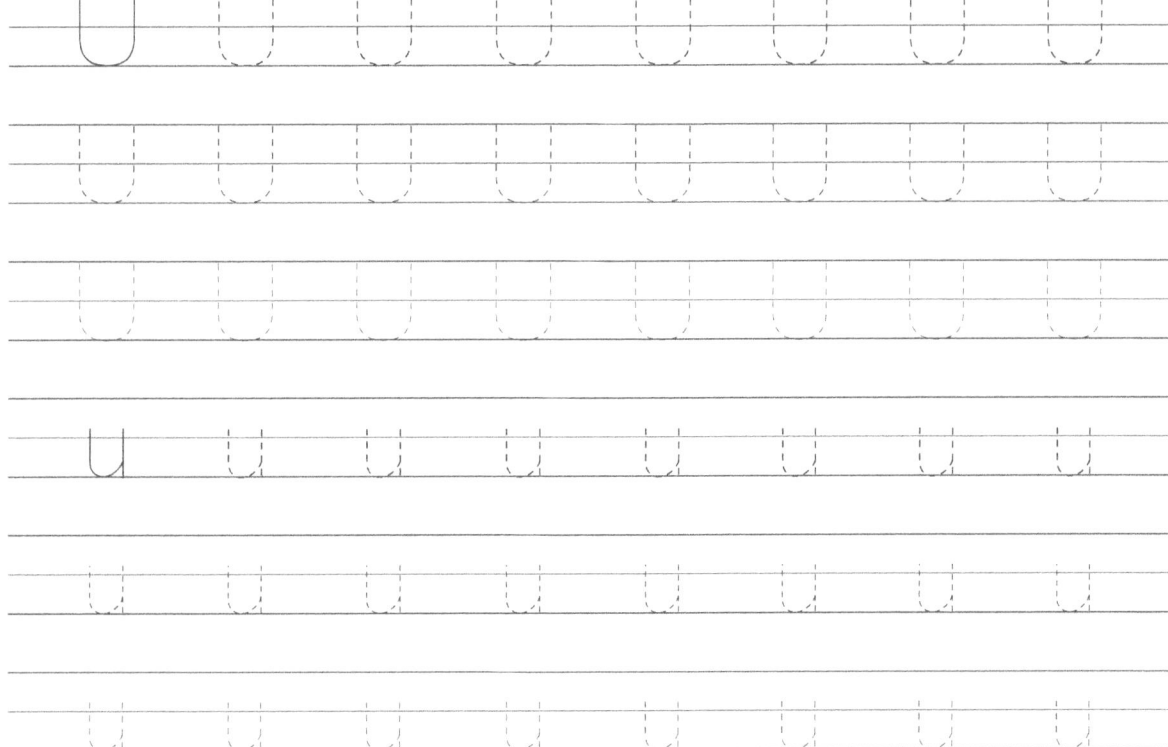

Trace Letter - V

Uppercase

Lowercase

V is for Vulture

Trace Letter - W

Uppercase

w
Lowercase

W is for Whale

Trace Letter - X

Uppercase

Lowercase

X is for X-ray fish

Trace Letter - Y

Uppercase

Lowercase

Y is for Yak

Trace Letter - Z

Uppercase

Lowercase

Z is for Zebra

www.ingramcontent.com/pod-product-compliance
Lightning Source LLC
Chambersburg PA
CBHW081159070526
44583CB00021B/2905